HUNTING AND FISHING

GOING BEAR HUNTING

BY FELIX PETERS

Gareth Stevens Publishing

Please visit our website, www.garethstevens.com. For a free color catalog of all our high-quality books, call toll free 1-800-542-2595 or fax 1-877-542-2596.

Cataloging-in-Publication Data
Names: Peters, Felix.
Title: Going bear hunting / Felix Peters.
Description: Buffalo, NY : Gareth Stevens Publishing, 2027. | Series: Hunting and fishing | Includes glossary and index.
Identifiers: ISBN 9781482482461 (pbk.) | ISBN 9781482482478 (library bound) | ISBN 9781482482485 (ebook)
Subjects: LCSH: Bear hunting--Juvenile literature.
Classification: LCC SK295.P484 2027 | DDC 799.2778--dc23

Published in 2027
Gareth Stevens Publishing
2544 Clinton Street
Buffalo, NY 14224

Portions of this work were originally authored by Tyler Omoth and published as *Bear Hunting*. All new material in this edition was authored by Felix Peters.

Designer: Joshua Olson
Editor: Noah Riccardi

Photo credits: Cover, p. 1 Sergey Uryadnikov/Shutterstock.com; p. 4 Wirestock Creators/Shutterstock.com; p. 7 A. G. Wallihan/Library of Congress; p. 8 andipantz/iStockphoto; p. 11 O2O Creative/iStockphoto ; p. 13 Zoran Orcik/Shutterstock.com; p. 14 Alexandre Boudet/Shutterstock.com; p. 17 Manamana/Shutterstock.com; p. 19 splendens/iStockphoto; p. 20 Anagramm/iStockphoto; p. 23 LuCaAr/iStockphoto; p. 24 Sandra San/Shutterstock.com; p. 27 Barashenkov Anton/iStockphoto; p. 29 Jake Lange/Shutterstock.com.

Printed in China

CPSIA compliance information: Batch #QS27GS: For further information contact Gareth Stevens at 1-800-542-2595.

TABLE OF CONTENTS

CHAPTER 1

FROM SURVIVAL TO SPORT

Humans have hunted bears since prehistoric times. People ate the bear meat. They also used the bear's heavy **pelt** to make warm clothing. Early hunters used spears and traps to take down these huge wild animals.

In medieval Europe, people began using dogs to help with hunting bears.

Forests are good places to find bears.

Weapons such as guns and bows also allowed hunters to shoot farther. Hunters no longer needed to get as close to bears. This helped make bear hunting much safer.

Most hunters today do not need the bear's meat or pelt for survival. However, the thrill of hunting bears for sport is still very much alive.

BEAR MEAT

Many hunters enjoy eating bear meat. The meat can vary in flavor depending on what the bear had been eating. Meat from a bear that ate mostly berries will taste different than meat from a bear that ate mostly fish. All bear meat should be cooked thoroughly.

Hunters in the late 1800s set traps to catch bears.

CHAPTER 2

WAYS TO HUNT

There are two main methods of bear hunting. They are called stalking and baiting. Hunters who stalk bears travel on foot. They watch for signs that bears are nearby. Common signs include scratch marks on trees, piles of **scat**, and prints in the mud or snow. Bears are often found in places with plenty of trees and shrubs.

Bears scratch tree bark to mark their territory.

They can also live in mountains and swamps. After hunters spot a bear, they **trail** the bear until there is a good opportunity for a shot.

Hunters who bait bears usually sit in a **tree stand**. They put out bait. The bait smells like something a bear would eat. Popular baits use the smell of black licorice and popcorn. Bears are attracted to these smells. They come closer to the hunter. As a result, it is easier for the hunter to get a good shot.

When hunters think they see a bear, they use their binoculars to get a better look. By confirming that it is a bear, hunters reduce the risk of hurting someone or

Hunters often practice their aim at shooting ranges before the hunting season begins.

shooting the wrong kind of animal. Hunters may also use rifle scopes to confirm targets. They may use laser range finders as well. The hunter points their range finder at a bear or at some other target.

The range finder measures the distance between the hunter and the target.

Bear hunters also choose between two kinds of weapons. Many use guns. Hunters who plan to shoot bears from a long distance often use high-powered rifles. Hunters who expect to get closer to bears tend to use shotguns instead. Shotguns do not have long ranges, but they are powerful. Hunters who bait bears often use shotguns.

Other hunters prefer the challenge of hunting with bows and arrows. There are many kinds of bows, including traditional bows and **compound bows**. A compound bow's **pulleys** make it easier for the

People who hunt with bows must train to build their muscles.

hunter to draw, or pull the string back. Each hunter should choose a bow that is powerful enough for the hunt but easy enough to draw and shoot.

A successful bear hunt with a bow and arrow requires a well-placed shot. It takes a lot of practice to learn how to aim.

CHAPTER 3

BEARS OF NORTH AMERICA

Hunters in North America pursue three main types of bears. Each kind presents a different set of challenges.

American black bears are the smallest bear species in North America. They range from 200 to 600 pounds (91 to 272 kg). Because of their size, these bears are the most popular type for bowhunting.

Black bears live all across North America.

Their varied diet also makes them prime targets for baiting. Black bears roam freely. They cover many miles each day. This can make them hard to track.

The grizzly bear is a member of the brown bear family. Grizzly bears live in the western United States and Canada.

POLAR BEARS

Polar bears are the largest species of bear in North America. But most hunters do not pursue them. For many years, only the Inuit people were allowed to hunt polar bears. Today, a few tags are released each season to non-Inuit hunters. These hunters are still required to have an Inuit guide. This guide receives any meat from a successful bear hunt.

A stream with salmon is a good spot to find grizzly bears.

These large bears often fish near rivers, lakes, and streams. Some grizzlies can weigh more than 800 pounds (363 kg). They can become very aggressive when threatened. They sometimes attack instead of running away.

Kodiak bears are the third major type of bear hunted in North America. Kodiak bears are another type of brown bear. They are found only in the Kodiak Islands in Alaska. Kodiak bears can be up to 10 feet (3 m) tall when standing on their hind legs. Adult males often weigh 1,000 pounds (454 kg).

Hunting Kodiak bears can be very dangerous. A hunter must stop the bear with just one shot. The animal's huge size makes this challenging. For this reason, hunting Kodiak bears with a bow and arrow is especially difficult.

Hunters must be cautious when approaching any kind of bear. Bears have

Bear hunters often hunt in groups for safety.

fairly good eyesight. But they use their powerful senses of hearing and smell to detect food and danger. A bear is likely to hear or smell a hunter before the hunter can see the bear. Hunters should make sure to stay downwind from a bear.

CHAPTER 4

HUNTING SAFELY

Bear hunters must know how to handle their guns or bows safely. A hunter should always treat a gun as if it were loaded. The gun's safety should be left on until the hunter is ready to fire. Hunters who use bows should keep their arrows in a quiver with a closable top until they are ready to shoot.

It is important to be careful when loading a rifle.

Hunting group members should create a plan so that each person knows where the others are at all times. Groups should plan where each member will go. And they should choose these positions carefully. Hunters should be positioned so they cannot accidentally shoot one another.

When tracking a bear, hunters must pay careful attention and not get too close. Bears can attack when aggravated. Wounded bears can be dangerous, too. If a bear attacks, hunters should not run. Instead, they should wave their arms, make noise, or aim for the bear's eyes.

Sows with cubs are especially dangerous. Hunters should never get

A mother bear can be very protective of her cubs.

between a sow and her cubs. The sow may see this as a threat. A hunter who does get between a sow and her cubs must not fight back. Instead, the hunter should play dead. The sow may stop attacking if she believes the threat is gone.

CHAPTER 5

RULES AND GUIDELINES

Governments create hunting seasons to help bears survive. Each state or province has its own hunting seasons. These seasons vary based on the type of bear. Hunters should be sure to know the rules for their area. They must also buy hunting licenses. A license tells the hunter what kind of bear is legal to hunt.

It is only legal to hunt grizzly bears in Alaska and in two provinces of Canada.

It also tells the hunter what size bears must be. Shooting the wrong type of bear will hurt the area's bear population. But following the guidelines helps keep the bear population stable. Money from license sales also helps fund programs that **preserve** the bears' natural **habitats**.

Hunters can help protect the bears' habitats. They should not leave anything behind at the hunting site. For example, they should pick up used rifle shells and shotgun slugs. Hunters should dispose of shells or slugs properly after they leave the hunting site. Otherwise, their shells and slugs could hurt the wild animals that live in the area.

When tracking a bear, a hunter often looks for paw prints.

Hunters should also track down any bears they shoot. Tracking a wounded animal can be difficult and dangerous. But hunters must not let wounded bears suffer. By being careful and following guidelines, hunters can help make sure that others will be able to enjoy hunting in the future.

FACT FILE

BEARS ON KODIAK ISLAND

Each year, many people visit Kodiak Island to hunt. This island is home to Kodiak bears. People are allowed to hunt them during two short periods each year. One is in the spring, and the other is in the fall. In the fall, hunters can find huge bears who have been feeding on salmon. In fact, the largest brown bear ever hunted was on Kodiak Island!

In 1952, a man named Roy Lindsley was part of a scientific **expedition**. While out near Karluk Lake, he spotted a huge Kodiak bear. Lindsley shot the animal with a rifle. Hunters often measure a bear's skull to track the animal's size. Lindsley's bear had a skull that was 17 15/16 inches (46.6 cm) long

Kodiak bears are some of the largest bears in the entire world.

and 12 13/16 inches (32.5 cm) wide. That set a world record for the largest brown bear ever hunted. As of 2025, that record still stood.

TEST YOUR KNOWLEDGE

Take this quiz to test your knowledge.

1. Write a letter to a friend explaining the main ideas of Chapter 2.

2. Would you rather hunt bears by baiting or stalking? Why?

3. Which type of bear is found only on islands in Alaska?

    A. grizzly bear
    B. Kodiak bear
    C. black bear

4. Why should a hunter try to stay downwind from a bear?

    A. so that the hunter can smell the bear
    B. so that leaves from nearby bushes will not get in the way
    C. so that the wind does not carry the hunter's scent to the bear

Answers can be found on page 32.

GLOSSARY

compound bows

Bows that use a series of pulleys.

expedition

A journey to find out about a place.

habitats

The type of places where plants or animals normally grow or live.

pelt

An animal's skin and fur.

preserve

To protect something so that it does not change.

pulleys

Wheels with grooves that ropes or chains run through.

scat

The waste of an animal.

sows

Female bears.

trail

To follow a scent or track in order to catch an animal.

tree stand

A platform that is perched up in a tree.

FOR MORE INFORMATION

BOOKS

Brach, Kyle. *Big Game Hunting*. Minneapolis, MN: Lerner Publications, 2024.

Kelly, Christa. *Alaska*. Minneapolis, MN: Abdo Publishing, 2025.

WEBSITES

Britannica Kids: American Black Bear
kids.britannica.com/kids/article/American-black-bear/638854
Learn more about American black bears.

National Geographic Kids: Alaska
kids.nationalgeographic.com/geography/states/article/alaska
Learn more about the home of Kodiak bears.

INDEX

Answer Key: 1. Answers will vary; 2. Answers will vary; 3. B; 4. C